"Greg has such an easy and clear writing
style. It made me want to really dig into the
world of graphic design."
Don Julien,
Filmmaker and photographer,
New York City

"*A Small Book About Design Craft and Practice*
by G. M. Donley is a concise, practical, and
indispensable guide, an essential tool
for any designer."
Suzanne DeGaetano,
Mac's Backs Books,
Cleveland Heights, Ohio

A SMALL BOOK ABOUT DESIGN CRAFT AND PRACTICE

My deepest thanks go to four people from whom I learned very much at the Cleveland Museum of Art—Thomas Barnard, Laurence Channing, Adele Silver, and Jeffrey Strean; and to three professors from my years of graduate work in a self-designed course of study in urban planning and aesthetics at Cleveland State University—the late Walter Leedy, Helen Liggett, and the late Norman Krumholz; and to Reed Simon, who asked me to teach his design class at Notre Dame College in the fall of 2021. And of course without my wife EB and the rest of our family, I wouldn't be doing any of this.

A Small Book About Design Craft and Practice
Published by Miscagon, Cleveland Heights, Ohio

Library of Congress Control Number: 2023902023

ISBN (print paperback): 979-8-9876725-0-1

Printed in USA
First edition February 2023

www.gmdonley.com

Contents

This book started as a series of talks and exercises for a course I taught as an adjunct professor at a local college. It was likely to be the only class in publication design that most of the students would ever take, so I set about trying to consolidate for them some key things I had learned over a few decades in various publishing and communications roles at the Cleveland Museum of Art and as a freelancer. Since there seemed to be no textbook for that, I put together a program that not only focused on design skills, but also emphasized something new designers often don't realize until they enter the workforce—that you need more than design talent and technical proficiency to be a successful working designer. You also need to embrace communication and collaboration, and you need to adopt production habits that help ensure a high-quality finished product.

College textbooks can be stunningly expensive—especially ones written by the professor and printed in very small quantities by the academic publishers who specialize in such things—so I initially planned to create just an online resource. Feedback from students, however, suggested that some sort of small printed item would be nice—in part to minimize having to toggle back and forth so much on a small laptop screen, but also just because people like physical books. That wasn't a hard sell. I like real books, too!

So I decided to use this project to explore the possibilities of print-on-demand publishing, whereby *a book of this type (no illustrations, no bleeds, small pages, and not very many of them) could be sold for well under $20, much less than it would cost just to photocopy the same material. Many of these students (and students in general) didn't have a lot of extra income, so I liked the idea that this might be the cheapest textbook they ever bought. I wouldn't try to cover everything—just fill in those gaps and describe some basic design strategies, and encourage people meanwhile to explore the many excellent books already written about typography, grids, illustration, user experience, brand identity, and everything else in the wonderful world of design.*

Once on that tack, I quickly decided that a small book about design craft and practice might not only provide the framework for a college class or maybe a series of workshops, but could also be something a working designer could use—particularly the kind of designer who may not initially have set out to do this kind of work but is doing it now and finds it fascinating and would like a little more grounding (myself 30 years ago, coincidentally).

So here it is. I'm not sure I'll teach a class again, but it's nice to have had that opportunity and to be able to pass on some knowledge . . . much respect to teachers—it's much less terrifying to just write a book!

THREE STRANDS

As someone who entered the design world almost by accident, I've always been a little envious of the people who seemed to have known from birth that some particular design discipline was their calling—the person who was just born to be a visionary architect, or a historically informed and aesthetically virtuosic typographer, or that industrial designer who somehow intuits how to create a race car that is both the fastest and the coolest-looking. Oh, to be blessed with such natural talent. And the clarity of vocational aspiration to get famous for it.

But I know it's not really like that, not for most people. As a long-time cyclist, I remember the first time someone referred to me as a "natural climber." I chuckled to myself. Clearly the commentator hadn't seen the preceding ten years of me trying every possible combination of techniques, equipment, training, nutrition, pacing strategies, and mental games to haul my butt up the hills a little more quickly. Truth was, I had only attained those "natural" gifts because I enjoyed cycling so much that I kept at it, both for a long time and with a consistent focus on getting better at it, aided by more experienced riders who could serve as mentors. Any able-bodied person who did that for a few years, trying to maximize strengths and minimize weaknesses, would end up as a half-decent bike rider. Still, like all competitive sports, cycling has a psychological element—why not let your competitors believe you have some kind of in-born genetic advantage over them? Cultivate a kind of mythology around these presumed natural gifts. It's probably like that for those "natural" designers too, right?

Of course there are genius designers out there, just as there are transcendently talented musicians, and rhetorically gifted novelists, and painters whose brushwork is so beautiful it makes you cry. And cyclists who combine the strength of a horse with the weight of a chickadee. If you're one of them, great—I look forward to shaking my head in appreciative astonishment the next time I see your work. Maybe I'll be lucky enough to grasp your hand someday so I can steal your DNA and send it off to the lab and clone you.

But alas, it turns out the genetic material of genius does not suffice.

First of all, talent alone doesn't cut it.
Yes, everybody in the Cleveland Orchestra
is super talented, but each one of those
musicians also spent decades building and
refining the craft of playing that instrument.
Practice, practice, practice. Who knows how
many supremely talented people are out there
who just didn't have the motivation or the
real-life opportunity to take it somewhere?
I'm not sure if that's the saddest thought
ever, or the most inspiring.

Furthermore, there just aren't that many
design geniuses in the world. Certainly
there aren't enough of them for every design
to show the "genius hand." And honestly,
even geniuses don't achieve genius in
everything they do, maybe not even in the
majority of what they do. A genius moment
is a rare thing, by definition.

Fortunately, we have craft.

Craft is a worthy end in itself. You could
make a good case that craft without
genius makes a better world than genius
without craft. A brilliant idea badly executed
may look exactly like a doltish idea badly
executed, because lousy craft makes genius

and banality equally moot. Meanwhile,
high craft without genius is still high craft.
Genius thoughts + great execution = Mozart
played by the Cleveland Orchestra. Dumb
thoughts + great execution = The Ramones.
Any idea + bad execution = Nobody
Remembers. The world is made better by
well crafted designs that succeed simply
because they do what they are designed
to do. That's enough. When a genius
moment comes along on top of high craft,
that's when you laugh out loud, or shed
a tear, or shake your head in appreciative
astonishment.

The more respect you give to craft, the
more you respect the value of formal design
education, which methodically instills the
most important principles of design craft,
day after day, project after project, semester
after semester. Practice, practice, practice.
Not only that, you also gain access to
mentors, rivals, and collaborators: the room
is probably full of other designers who
can inspire you, challenge you, frustrate
you, baffle you, and convince you of your
genetic superiority and/or inferiority, and
thus help prepare you for what lies ahead if
you intend to spend a lot of time and effort
designing things.

That said, formal design education doesn't really seem to prepare designers for the back-and-forth of working with clients who expect to have input but are not designers or design educators and don't already know what you're talking about when you reference Paul Rand or allude to x-height. That's something most people learn about on the job, and it can be a bit jarring, especially to introverts (a term that would describe a lot of designers). Design is not just you working in your studio dreaming up awesome things, it's you and your client making something together. If you want to create awesome stuff in your studio by yourself without having to think about someone else's ideas, then go to it. But that's not really what a designer does. That's what an artist does. If that's you, congratulations, you're an artist! But if you want to help other people solve their problems, if you want external assignments that test your ingenuity, if you love making the practical beautiful and the beautiful practical, then design is for you.

Design always taps the designer's creative resources, but it isn't really self-expression. It's a kind of collaborative product melding functional imperatives,

cultural priorities, and aesthetic choices, all
tempered by practical constraints: budget,
space, time. Think of such constraints
as a liberating limitation. Shakespeare
managed to do okay with 14 lines of iambic
pentameter. He wrote more than a hundred
sonnets and was never heard to say "I
demand fifteen syllables per line and 18
lines, or I quit." A sonnet is a sonnet.

But to embrace parameters, you have to
know them. The time to find out that your
assignment was to write a sonnet is not after
you have already composed *King Lear*.

Now, in your defense, maybe your
client never said the thing was supposed to
be a sonnet, or even actively tried to avoid
saying anything specific. Lesson learned for
you—it's in your interest as a designer, and
ultimately in the client's interest, too, to find
out. It's on you. That's why the very first step
in a successful design project doesn't have
anything to do with how good you are with
color and line and type and composition. It
has to do with how good an interviewer you
are, how good a listener, how good you are at
articulating what you think the client wants
so you can find out if you've got it right
before taking you both down a long, wrong
path. When you get that communication

right, it frees your mind for the creative
part—and that's when beautiful things can
happen. The interview informs the craft.

What does good craft look like? Think
of a well-made chair. It's strong. The lines
of it are appealing. The joints are clean. It's
comfortable to sit in. It looks right in the
room where it's placed. In graphic design?
Things line up. The pictures look great. Type
is legible and attractive. The paper looks and
feels right. The colors work together. The
composition illuminates the content. Bleeds
and folds and trims are precise. Simply put,
it feels well conceived and well made.

For the purposes of this brief volume
and its handful of exercises, the craft
of design intertwines three strands: one
strand is about a process of ongoing
communication and collaboration; another
is about principles of composition,
structure, and visual meaning; and the
third is about production habits that help
ensure that all the work that went into the
first two strands isn't squandered by poor
execution. Braid them well together and
you should be able to consistently produce
solid design craft. Maybe people look at
those results and declare it to be genius.
Just smile and go about your craft.

THE
INTERVIEW

Write out on a piece of paper, or tap into
your phone, or type on your computer these
four words: audience, outcome, message,
tone. Sit down with your client at the outset
of a project and don't leave until you have
answers to these four questions:

Who is the **audience** for the planned
design? Are there multiple audiences?

What is the desired **outcome**? What do
you want the audience to do in response to
experiencing this design?

What **message** will encourage them to do
that? The message can literally be a line
of text, as in advertising, or it can be more
implicit, as in a book design that amplifies
the editorial content in a particular way
and thus encourages the reader to subscribe
to the ideas being presented, perhaps
envision this book occupying a place of
prominence of a coffee table or bookshelf.

What kind of **tone** is appropriate in
this context? Forceful and authoritative?
Humorous? Cajoling? Nurturing? What
tone will likely appeal to this audience
around this message?

To start with a concrete example, let's dissect this book. Who is it for? When developing this idea, I envisioned two readers: one would be a student in a college class using the book's practical exercises over the course of a semester, with the professor supplementing with other content as desired; and the other would be the person who has ended up as the in-house designer for an organization or as a sole practitioner but who has not had the benefit of much formal design education, and is seeking to learn a bit more. So this small book concisely gathers very basic conceptual and practical material in one place along with a few exercises that model real-world experience. College textbooks and design books in general can be frightfully expensive. This book is really cheap.

The intended outcome is that the book is adopted by these readers as part of the author's personal campaign to democratize design craft to a broader population so that more people get to live with better design. The message is that design is a demanding and complex endeavor, but you don't need to be a genius to produce beautiful craft. And the tone is informal, a bit irreverent, intended to demystify.

It's frequently the case—almost always—that the client enters into the project without having pre-articulated the answers to these questions. They may not even realize they haven't made their minds up about certain things. Your interview must lead them through the process of spelling out exactly what it is they're hoping to achieve. At this juncture they may be forced to make some decisions.

Say you're designing a car. A tiny 2-seat sports car might not work that great for hauling refrigerators. But the panel truck that can carry the refrigerator won't likely be much fun to drive and it definitely won't be easy on the gasoline budget. One design can't really do both. Which one is it going to be? Or maybe you have a line of clothing. Is it for hipster urbanites or the country club set? Distressed denim or pastel polos?

The client may start off by saying their product is so great that everyone should love it, that the target audience is everyone. Here's where you as the interviewer/ designer can be very helpful by saying "That may be true, but for the purpose of the ads we're going to develop together, we'll need to focus on a potential customer you think is a particularly good fit." Then talk about what message and tone should work for that group to get them to try out a line of clothing that is new to them. Don't stop talking about it until you have agreement on the four questions for that audience.

Then, if it seems appropriate, ask if there's a secondary customer for whom we could answer the same questions. Do you need a primary campaign and a secondary one? And then, of course, consider the budget: can you really afford to do two campaigns at first, or had we better focus on just one for now? You need to force decisions. Without those decisions, you'll likely be designing and redesigning and redesigning, and the client may begin to wonder why you can't get it right.

The other interesting thing that often happens as part of this interview process is that, in addition to getting the answers to those critical questions, you get to know the client better, and you come to understand their products and hopefully to share their enthusiasm about those products, which can help you get a sense of what might excite potential customers or audiences. And that, of course, will benefit the whole project.

Really understanding the product and its users always benefits the project.

Sometimes a client will show up to an initial interview with a sample of a brochure they got somewhere and will essentially ask you to replicate it for their product. Rather than simply saying "no problem" or "no, that's stupid," take this as a chance for another interview around this concrete design. It's a great opportunity to move beyond abstract principles and critique an actual, physical design object: What about this piece do they think works well? Who does the intended audience seem to be? What is the message? The tone? What do they think the brochure gets people to do? Maybe you do end up copying the format. Or maybe, after talking it through, the client says, "You know what, my product and audience are a little different, so let's look at some other ways to do this." Whatever. Now you have more information, and you've established a viable collaboration.

With that information in hand, agree on a strategy and a timetable, shake hands, and set up a meeting to review some design sketches. Now you get to actually design something.

A
FEW
KEY
REFERENCES

There would not be not much point in paraphrasing here the wisdom found in the many very fine books that have already been written about design. You should read them yourself. Start with Michael Bierut's *79 Short Essays on Design,* or some of Ellen Lupton's practical guides. Follow your curiosity. But there are a few books you ought to have on your desk for reference. Get Robert Bringhurst's *The Elements of Typographic Style.* Get another modest book with almost the same title, Strunk and White's *The Elements of Style*—because even if you think you're just a designer, you still need to understand how writing works. You can get both of these

online, or if you're lucky to have second-
hand bookstores around, go browsing
and you may find what you need locally.
These publications have been around for
decades, and older editions still pertain.
Get a dictionary, maybe a thesaurus, too.
You don't need to own a book about grids,
but you should read one (Timothy Samara's
Making and Breaking the Grid is popular).
To keep up on current trends as well as
graphic design history, bookmark the
American Institute of Graphic Art's website
and subscribe to the free online newsletter
Eye on Design: eyeondesign.aiga.org/. You
don't need to be an AIGA member.

If your client already has an editorial
"house style," find out what it is and use
it (even if it seems as if many of their own
staff don't use it themselves). If they don't
already have a house style, note that, while
the AP style is often used as a default, you
do not have to walk that well-worn path.
The AP style was developed decades ago by
the Associated Press for transmission over
old pre-digital wire machines, and part of
the point of it was to save on key strokes
and make life a tiny bit easier for the poor
beleaguered person in the newspaper office
who had to retype what was spit out on the
endless paper roll by the black steel beast
mumbling intermittently in the corner.
Since it had to be retyped anyway, the
person doing the typing could translate the
copy back out of AP ticker-tape style on the
fly, into whatever style their publication
used, in the process remedying some
of AP style's shortcomings—things like
restoring serial (Oxford) commas, spelling
out abbreviated months and days, and
so on. Truth is, AP style can look pretty
clunky on the page in set type, which is
why you'll see very few nice magazines or
books using it. *The Chicago Manual of Style*
provides a more attractive alternative. Many

publications use Chicago (also referred to
by editors as CMoS) as a starting point,
adding customizations to fit their own
content and audiences. Many libraries offer
free access to the online version, and you
can often find that big orange book in used
bookstores, too. If that's on your desk, then
when clients come over, and you suggest
the typography and editorial style follow the
Chicago Manual of Style, you can hand them
that weighty object and they'll appreciate
the gravity of your recommendation.

THE
FORMULA

Ha-ha. There is no formula. You can close
the book and go home now.

Still here? Okay, there are some concepts to
understand that can help any design succeed.
Here they are: Be disciplined. Break rules.
Limit the number of type sizes. Change scale.
Be predictable. Defy expectations. Don't
disorient your audience. Throw a curve ball.

    This bipolar dynamic goes by many
names, but what it is about essentially is
making sure that your design has both
a degree of predictability—for ease of
navigation, clarity of communication, and
for instilling a sense of confidence in your

users that they understand what's going on—
and elements of surprise that play off the
predictability to offer moments of discovery
and delight. Structure supports ornament.
The mechanical frames the organic. The
back beat underpins the improvisation. The
grid grounds the things that break out of it.
For the purposes of this discussion, we're
going to call these two factors *coherence* and
complexity. If you manage to hit the sweet
spot of coherence and complexity, the users
of your design will find it intuitive and
easy to understand, and also enlivened with
surprise and delight. So how do these work
together?

It's possible to create good music that has no rhythm and structure, but there's a reason that most songs have a beat you can pick up on right away, and some kind of form that helps the listener follow along with the story being told. A coherent structure—distinguished by regularity, repetition of forms, consistency of scale—simplifies the usability of anything you make. It builds in a certain amount of predictability and communicates a sense of order. As a user, you know where you are, and you have a good hunch about how to navigate. Unsurprisingly, a host of studies across creative disciplines show that people favor coherent designs over unstructured ones, whether you're talking about magazines or city parks or symphonies.

Coherence may set the mind at ease, but it is not necessarily very interesting in itself—adding complexity sparks sensory interest and requires the user to analyze information, perhaps even to decipher clues. An engaged mind is inspired to continue to explore and becomes invested in the interaction.

The better-versed a user is with the language of a particular form of design expression, the higher their tolerance of

and desire for increased complexity; by
contrast, novice users may respond best to
relatively non-complex designs. That's why
avant-garde and experimental art forms
tend to have audiences of the most seasoned
and literate aficionados—people who
have developed a taste for dissonance and
challenging forms.

It is possible to serve more than one
user: if the basic functions of a design are
accessible to a novice, that doesn't mean
the same design can't also include more
sophisticated content to inspire those whose
literacy is already advanced. Beethoven,
Frida Kahlo, Frank Lloyd Wright, Toni
Morrison—there are plenty of examples of
work that is accessible to the uninitiated
and also rewards repeated experiences for
the most advanced expert. But hitting all
those notes is not easy. Somebody like
J. S. Bach may be able to attain
transcendent creativity on a frequent basis.
For the rest of us, if we just make sure to
nail the solid craft, the users of a design
will be satisfied and happy, if not always
launched into profound rapture. The first
job is the well crafted design.

It can be enlightening to study the
role of structure and form in various other

creative disciplines, especially if you are
someone for whom analogies provide a
useful way to understand things. This kind
of knowledge of other fields can be useful
in discussing concepts with your clients
also—to say that what you're doing is like
the chorus/verse/chorus structure of a pop
song, or that the reason you're putting a
particular element in a particular place is
the same reason the church presides over
the town square, or that a carefully paced
sequence of pages is like a Hitchcock movie
setting up the unsuspecting audience for
the sudden surprise. Much like that verse/
chorus/verse song might have a bridge
section that temporarily departs from
the predictability of the song just as the
listener is getting used to it, your designs
can throw in a surprise every once in a
while, too. Obviously you can't get much
of a surprise at the beginning, because
there's no expectation to disrupt yet, so this
is something to do after you've established
and used your disciplined structure for
a while. Then jump out of the shadows
and yell BOO! Do it in specific places for
dramatic effect.

Different forms of creative product
engage different human senses in different

ways and combinations and at different
scales in relation to the human body—but
the principles of intentional structure and
intentional departure from regularity apply
across all creative disciplines.

What structure to use? Rule of thirds?
Golden Section? Tic Tac Toe? It doesn't
matter. Just establish a structure and stick
to it. That said, sometimes the nature of
the content might suggest a certain grid.
Designing a weekly calendar? One of
the frameworks you might logically try
would be a seven-column grid. Anyway,
you can guess six columns probably ain't
gonna work, unless nothing ever happens
on Mondays. And even then, it's worth
remembering that readers really expect
calendars to show all seven days of the
week, so you're welcome to confound that
expectation, but do so with your eyes open.
You'd be advised to give the audience
an equally clear way to understand your
graphic presentation of a week.

It's not that grids are indispensable
in all situations—a simple rectangular
composition like a poster can certainly be
done by intuition without much thought to
an underlying framework—but using a grid
will almost never make a design worse. I

don't know how many times I opened up
a designer's InDesign file to find elements
placed with little regard to the grid—and
yet that particular page or poster or ad
worked just fine even so. But the longer
and more complex a publication is, the
more important it is to establish some sense
of regularity and rhythm. You can even
work backwards—compose that poster or ad
spontaneously then use that composition
as the basis for a grid. Place the grid
lines, then make a few minor moves to get
everything to line up. It looks sloppy when
things don't quite align. Using grids is the
easiest way to avoid that problem.

So make a grid. It may feel limiting—
and it is—but also liberating. And it's not
uncreative. Experiment with even and odd
numbers of columns, different divisions of
the vertical space, ways of assigning zones
of the grid to particular purposes. What
happens when the structure is symmetrical?
Asymmetrical? When the grid increments
are smaller as opposed to larger? Observe
what happens, then figure out how to use
it. Make it, follow it, thoughtfully break it
on occasion.

This book, being only 4 x 7 inches
finished size, uses a very simple grid—one

column per page, equal margins all around, and a single horizon line across the middle that is used only when new sections begin. A larger page size would likely have more columns and horizontal increments.

As for incorporating complexity— take this as an opportunity to reinforce meaning. Once the predictable structure is established, anything that departs from that predictability will inevitably draw attention to itself. Therefore make sure those off-grid moments are treated as opportunities to communicate something important. Same with big scale changes. Be intentional about it. Use what you know about what's important and meaningful to this audience (find out more if you need to) and decide what elements to incorporate in order to encourage exploration in ways that will resonate with those users: meaningful images at prominent places in the structure, historical context, cultural cues, decoration that plays off structure and helps set an intentional tone, color and texture that support the theme.

Methodically go though the project, testing constantly against the audience, objective, message, and tone, until you're done. Done getting started.

DO YOUR GENIUS THING

Now I know I just got done saying there aren't enough geniuses to go around, but that doesn't mean some genius moments can't come from us non-geniuses.

Everybody, designer or not, has some unusual way of seeing the world, or a particularly sharp eye for some kind of information or imagery, a distinct way of combining elements and playing them off each other, a certain sense of humor. We're going to call that your creative personality. It's how you respond to things, how you choose to present ideas, your aesthetic taste, a sort of common thread that a careful observer would be able to discern running through your work. While design work is less about self-expression than collaborative expression, you can and should tap your creative personality to make your design work better.

When it comes to composition, anything you may have learned in a drawing or painting class can be applied in designing a publication. Composition is composition. It's about making conscious choices: What marks are where? What is the textural quality of those marks? What's light? What's dark? How do colors work with each other? What recognizable images are there and what meanings might they bring to the picture? You as a designer are responsible for all of that.

As you work with publishing materials, it becomes clear that most elements do more than one job. Body text is both verbal meaning and visual texture. Headlines are words with meaning, and navigational signposts, and abstract shapes. Illustrations are color, shape, and texture and also the whatever the picture signifies to the reader. This multitasking characterizes the experience of publications no matter what, so take charge of it. Hear every voice and give each a role in the composition.

Realize that you're doing something pretty complicated here: you're composing spaces using type and color and images and texture with an awareness not only of the visual aesthetics but also of the meanings of the images and the words, and you're integrating all of that with a particular audience in mind, and using an intentional message and tone all working toward your client's desired outcome. And you're consciously managing all of this through a coherent, intuitively navigable framework that has elements of complexity and surprise designed to engage and delight the audience. That's a lot of balls in the air.

So take a pause. Let the balls stay frozen in place while you do something else, then come back and review the whole thing with an eye for the little details you might have missed. Refine it. Clean it up. Clean it up again. Make sure all the balls are accounted for and put them away. Time to share it with your client.

A common variation on this process is to present three alternatives. This can be especially useful in developing something like an ad campaign that at first may be somewhat open-ended in terms of message and tone—by presenting three alternatives, you can try different messages, each with its own appropriate tone and graphic elements, then you and the client can decide which way to go. Sometimes you might end up with a hybrid of a couple ideas. That's fine as long as things don't get muddled. Discussing alternatives with the client shows respect for their desire to have a role in developing the concepts, it helps ensure everyone feels invested, and it can be a good way to save some time by exploring alternatives up front rather than in sequence.

What can be dangerous is using the "choice of three" process to try to fast-

track the designer's favorite idea. That
is, the designer presents the concept they
love, plus two vastly inferior alternatives,
assuming the client will cast aside the crap
options and get behind the good one. The
client will instead almost invariably either
choose one of the disfavored ideas or insist
upon incorporating elements of all three.
Then what are you going to say? That you
presented sucky ideas on purpose? And
charged the client to do that?

Never present anything you can't live
with. It's better to leave good ideas on the
"spare parts" table than to have too few.
In fact, you should be happy that you can
generate more good ideas than you could
ever use. That should be your goal. After
you've had lots of experience of not using
every good idea, you'll get used to that
as just part of the process and it won't
make you too sad. And who knows, maybe
someday, that old idea sitting back there in
the corner, that might work over here . . .

A SIDE NOTE ABOUT SKILLS
If you're like most of us, during the process
of refining your project, you'll periodically
find yourself mumbling to yourself "Dang,
I wish I knew how to . . ."

A couple of generations ago, a graphic
designer had to be good with an X-Acto
knife and drafting tools, to know how a
stat camera worked and how to scale color
transparencies for reproduction and where
to send them off to have color separation
films made. These days you need a decent
computer setup and you need to have
and know how to use at least InDesign
and Photoshop and Illustrator. Not
cheap, especially if you can't get student
or academic rates. In another couple
decades you will probably need to know
something else. It won't do you any good
to insist on using Freehand just because
you invested time and money in it 30 years
ago. Whatever the era, you always need to
know how to use the basic tools that are in
current use, period.

And of course, many skills you
learned in school or on your own will
become obsolete. It's possible to teach
yourself new skills or update existing ones
by using online tutorials and/or joining
local user groups, if you have any in your
area. Or take a class. Anyway, prepare for
a lifetime of learning new stuff.

No matter what your skills, there
may be cases when you decide to tap the

expertise of, for instance, your friend who is a bona fide Illustrator whiz when you get to that "I wish I knew how to . . ." moment. Don't be shy about that. Find a way to trade if you can't afford to pay subcontractors. You don't want a nice idea to be sunk by bad execution.

These days, the role of graphic designers in web and online media is mostly to prep images and text for a content management system—usually a matter of devising workflows to produce images at specific pixel dimensions and perhaps copying and pasting a bit of html code. Dabbling in web design can be fun, but any task beyond your current level of expertise is best passed on to a real web designer when paying clients are involved.

There can be a kind of mythology around creative projects that devalues iteration. Maybe it's because the designer got super excited about some idea and they're reluctant to expose it to the possibility of modification. Maybe they don't want to seem to be encouraging clients to keep changing their minds. Maybe it starts to seem to be like asking for design by committee, leading to some sort of ineffectual mediocrity that excels at nothing. Or maybe the designer is just lazy and/or arrogant and doesn't feel like revising anything. Be strong. Strength means embracing iteration for what it is: the best opportunity at this point in the process to make the design better. Throw some energy into it.

Also have some sympathy for the client, who may, like most people, have a harder time than you do visualizing things until they have something concrete in front of them. Respect that. People's brains and eyes work in different ways. So sit down with the client and the draft and mark it up, cut it up, tape it together, whatever works. It's no big deal to whip up another version. You like that. You're a designer.

Agree to come back at a set time with the next iteration, and then to at least one more meeting for final design approval, allowing realistic time for whatever pre-press or other production is needed before the project gets sent off to its printer, fabricator, etc. Sticking to a firm schedule helps your client clarify priorities and make timely decisions, and it shows professional respect to anyone downstream of you.

FILE SETUP AND PRODUCTION

For all your sophisticated ideas to successfully get across to your audience (or even to your client), everything has to work right mechanically. You cannot ignore this. Mechanical problems can negate creative genius quicker than a power failure would dampen a Spinal Tap reunion.

The following processes are described for graphic designers using InDesign and Photoshop as of 2022. No doubt the processes will change over time, but there are some things that will not change: to avoid discovering a disaster when a publication arrives from the printer,

documents need to be set up with proper
bleed and trim areas; images need to be of
adequate resolution and in the proper color
space for the size and type of reproduction;
and fonts need to be handled properly.

Beyond simple disaster-avoidance,
there are a number of processes that exploit
the logic of how page layout and image-
editing software and hardware work today
(and probably will in the future) in order to
streamline workflows for the designer and
avoid mistakes and glitches that can arise
from doing too much hand-work in tasks
where the computer can do it better (with
some purposeful human guidance).

Before opening or creating any file
Start InDesign

Under PREFERENCES Leave all the
defaults alone except under advanced
Type: set small cap size to 80% if the font
doesn't have native small caps. Make sure
typographer's quotes are turned on.

Under WINDOW, select CONTROL so the
control palette shows up at the top of the
document (saves a lot of menu pulling later).

Create a new document
Type a few characters anywhere. Once you
do this, any new type you add will default to
the font and size you define here.

File/Document Setup/Bleed and Slug: set
bleed to .125 (all 4 sides), the US printing
standard. The .125 accounts for inevitable
variations in mechanical trims (such as in
thick saddle-stitched magazines), so don't put
any important edge within .125 of a trim line.

Under WINDOW open the LINKS palette.
Click the upper right corner options box
and select Panel Options. Check the boxes
for Actual PPI and Effective PPI.

Always use Paragraph Style Sheets
As you are developing your design, create
style sheets under WINDOW/STYLES/
Paragraph Styles. This book, for example,
uses a handful of styles: body copy without
indent, body copy with indent, body copy
with a drop cap, body copy bulleted list,
all cap section heading, page number,
credits, cover title. Every bit of type in your
publication should be defined by a style.
This is so that if, for example, you are in the
late stages of a 128-page annual report and
for some reason you need to change all the
subheads, but no other type, from Helvetica
to Palatino, you can do that by revising the
specs of that style sheet (takes 30 seconds
and automatically finds every instance of
that style throughout the publication), as
opposed to needing to manually go through
all 128 pages and find every example (could
take hours and you can easily miss some
instances). Working through paragraph
styles also guarantees that your typography
has a high level of consistency throughout
the design—the kind of background structure
that helps people navigate with confidence.
Finally, if you plan to make an e-book
version of your publication, having all the
content style-sheeted is a prerequisite.

Always use Master Pages

The reasons to use master pages are similar
to the reasons to use style sheets: with a
small amount of up-front planning you can
make it much faster and easier to change
course later, and you automatically build
in a level of consistency to your publication
that makes it more navigable. Under the
WINDOW/PAGES palette you will find
a default master page called A-Master.
Double-click on this master to edit it. For
example, you can alter the margins and
make it a certain number of columns.
Then rename it accordingly (retaining the
initial letter, which InDesign requires),
for example "A-3 column." Anything you
put on this master page will show up on
every page in your document to which this
master is applied—text, images, grid lines,
and so on. It's a good idea to add a certain
number of horizontal grid lines that divide
up the space vertically in some logical way.
Place the top arrow tool in the ruler along
the top and drag down to where you want
the grid line to be. Fine-tune its position by
editing the numbers in the control palette.

This is also the time to add page
numbers, if desired. To do that, draw a
text box with the T tool, then under TYPE

select INSERT SPECIAL CHARACTER/
MARKER/Current page number. A letter
"A" will be inserted in the box on the
master, and this letter will be replaced by
the current page number on that page of
the actual document. Decide what font and
size you want the page numbers to be by
editing that letter A and then create a new
paragraph style for page numbers.

Create any new master pages you like
in that manner. Note that if the new master
is based on [None] that page will start from
scratch, but if it is based on a master you
have already created, it will start by copying
everything on that master.

Always File/Place Images rather than drag-and-drop

People often drag and drop images to sketch
ideas, but dragged/dropped images are only
72 ppi, and printing generally requires 300
ppi. To save having to fix all that later (or
worse, having a bad image sneak into a
printed product), keep all your final images
in one location and let the InDesign file link
to them by placing rather than dragging from
Photoshop or Illustrator. FILE/PLACE or
command+D (Mac) or CTRL+D (Windows).
This "real printing" workflow also allows you

or another person to work on the images independently, and the latest version will automatically load into the InDesign file (as long as the image file name isn't changed).

Package the Project
The FILE/PACKAGE option in InDesign makes a copy of the InDesign file and a copy of every image and font used in the InDesign file, and saves them all in one place of your choosing. You can then move that package around via cloud or flash drive or SD card or whatever, without the danger of some key part of the project getting lost or deleted by accident. Also, when it comes time for pre-press image production, the modifications you make to images for this one project won't affect the original images which may be needed for other projects at different resolutions, etc. It's a good practice to immediately close the previous InDesign file and move it into an "old" folder so it does not accidentally get opened instead of the current working file.

Image production
Go through the entire publication starting with page 1. Open each image (select image, Edit/Open With [select Photoshop]). In

Photoshop, size the image so it is slightly over 300 ppi (up to 350 or so) at the reproduction size (effective ppi—this is why you set up your links palette to show effective and actual ppi). If the image starts out much below that, reduce the reproduction size or get a better image. Convert to the printer's color profile (for typical US sheetfed printing, use Coated GRAcol 2006 from the standard list, or something else if the printer requests it) by selecting Edit/Convert to Profile in Photoshop. Next—judgment call based on the character of the image—sharpen a bit (unsharp mask starting with 5/50/100). Beware that too much sharpening can create banding effects in smooth tonal gradations, so for images like that, lay off the sharpening. For color correction, the idea in general is to match the original art as closely as possible (which is fun because some originals have color intensity that is beyond the capabilities of CMYK printing). Anything that was not a PSD is saved as a PSD (no image deterioration with re-saving and allows turning layers on/off from InDesign) and the link is updated from the InDesign document.

File prep and delivery for printer
Once the final copy edits and the image

production are done, create a "To printer" folder and export a pdf into that folder using the printer's preferred distiller setting with crop marks and bleeds. Some printers will request separate page outputs for some jobs, in which case they will supply a file format and naming convention for that.

Carefully examine these high-resolution to-printer pdfs to be sure fonts are behaving as expected and to verify that nothing that's supposed to be on the pages has disappeared. The actual printing plates come directly from these files, so if there is any problem here, it will be there. It's a good time to zoom way in to ensure that any clipping path outlines are nice and clean and that overlapping elements are layered as you planned. If anything is wrong, fix it now and you'll save on paying for an additional round of printer proofs.

Printed Color: Managing expectations and avoiding disappointment
The ability to create mass quantities of beautiful printed color publications as easily as we can today is taken for granted, but it really is pretty amazing. Think about how color prints are made by hand: two or three or more blocks of wood or linoleum

or stone are set up so each one prints a
single color, and the printmaker works out
a way to line them up super precisely . . .
with commercial printing, we have figured
out how to do that at an industrial scale
and how to apply what we know about how
color works to print images that look very
much like the photographs that are used to
make the printing plates. And that process
begins with photographs that reproduce
what was in front of the camera with
incredible fidelity. Decent color printing
in mass quantities has existed only since
the 1930s or so, and the level of quality we
currently expect has existed only for the past
couple of decades, since the whole workflow
"went digital" from digital cameras through
Photoshop to computer-controlled color-
management systems and printing presses.

But still, artists and photographers
and designers are picky and we can't help
but notice that printed images don't look
exactly like the photographs, and that the
photographs don't look exactly like the
original things they were trying to capture.
Why not?

Part of the reason is that a lot is lost
when we go from four dimensions to two,
and from a pair of eyes to pixels. Human eyes

can perceive a very wide range of contrast and
color as the 120 million rods and 6 million
cones in each eye capture information on
the fly, with the pupils and lenses constantly
adjusting to changing light and points of
focus, plus stereoscopic depth. A camera
captures a small slice of time, squeezes
four dimensions down to two, and makes a
decision about what parts of the image are
exposed correctly and what will be too light
and too dark—all things the human eye can
do better. At the same time, the camera
can do things the eye can't, such as capture
information outside the visible spectrum
(UV and IR) and record the high-resolution
images designers use in publications.

The rest of it has to do with color
gamut, which is the outer limit of color
that can be achieved by a given technology.
A lot of intensity is lost when a light-based
transmissive image (as captured by a camera
and seen on a monitor) is translated to a
pigment-based reflective image printed on
paper. High-end fine-art prints made for
exhibitions are typically made using devices
that use 6 or 8 inks to achieve super-rich
color and density, so they look great but still
offer less intensity than a monitor. Mass-
scale printing—offset lithography—uses only

four inks, which further limits the range
of color intensity as compared to a fine art
print, transparency, screen image, or of
course, the original scene.

The best practices for designing color
publications, therefore, are all about
trying to get the very most out of the printing
technology available, with the understanding
that offset lithography can't give you what
you see with your eye, or on your camera, or
on your monitor, or in your fine-art print.
Managing color in a print workflow is about
setting realistic expectations in the first
place, then adopting measures to meet those
expectations.

The best way to look at these strategies
is that if you accept that a certain printing
technology can do only certain things, then
you can adapt your approach so that the
viewer's subjective impression of the printed
image within the context of that publication
will be positive. Holding the page that has
a printed image of the Vincent van Gogh
painting up against the actual painting
would show a distressing loss of color
intensity, but within the context of a printed
book being read in somebody's living room,
where the person's eyes have adjusted to the

light and the printed images are understood in the context of the other printed images in the book, it can work well enough.

In the physics of light and color, light-based additive color (the RGB that your eye perceives, that your camera captures, and your monitor displays) communicates a much broader range of intensity than the pigment-based color used in any printing. In additive color, all colors blended yield white, and the absence of any color is black. Subtractive color is the opposite: white is the absence of color and black is attained by mixing the primary print colors (Cyan, Magenta, and Yellow); in practice, the blacks attained this way prove to be weak. An additional problem is that small type printed using three inks is fuzzy at best and completely illegible if the printing plates get out of register. Both problems are addressed by adding one more ink: pure black (referred to as K in the CMYK color setup), which adds depth and "punch" to images and provides crisp black type even if the C, M, and Y plates get out of register.

Given that CMYK is an imperfect compromise in the first place, there is still a wide range of quality attainable through CMYK-based commercial printing based on

the type of paper used and the equipment
used to print on it. Bright white coated
(glossy) paper printed using high-end sheetfed presses (Heidelberg being the most
famous) can attain the highest levels of
intensity and contrast and subtlety, while at
the other end of the quality range, web-
offset printing on newsprint is, to put it
mildly, somewhat limited in its capability
to faithfully render an image. Envision a
big roll of toilet paper on which every drop
of ink spreads and blurs, a phenomenon
known as dot gain.

Designers and publishers and printers
deal with all these possibilities digitally
through a system of color profiles that are
based on the capabilities of various printing
technologies. Photoshop has a huge list of
profiles that can be assigned that represent a
wide range of printing presses and papers. If
you open up Color Management, you'll see
"Working Space"and "Destination Space."
Working space is what you see on your
monitor while working (RGB); destination
space represents how this publication will
end up being printed (usually CMYK but
also possibly an RGB space for a fine art
Epson printer or similar that might be
used for making one-off prints for an art

exhibition—these take many minutes per print and thus are not practical for any kind of quantity printing). If you want your working space to look nearly as bad as what will happen when it's printed and thus head off potential disappointment, set the working space to sRGB, affectionately referred to in the industry as "sh***y RGB." For fine art prints, you can and should load a profile specific to the device and paper to get the most out of those resources.

A useful Photoshop tool for "problem child" images whose color gamut far exceeds the capabilities of the destination printing technology is to go to the View menu, check Proof Colors, then select Gamut Warning. This will gray out portions of the image that are beyond the range of what the selected printing technology can do. With Gamut Warning on, you can subtly adjust saturation and vibrancy under Image/Adjust until all the gray warning area is gone. This is a good alternative to just closing your eyes and hoping the result isn't too bad when you actually get to ink on paper. Ask your printer what setting you should use for your destination profile, and ask them to send you the distiller job options file for making your final printer-ready output. Load this through InDesign by selecting File/Adobe PDF Presets/Define/Load and select the job options file the printer sent you.

Do all that, and assuming your workflow includes receiving color proofs from the printer, you should find that these proofs are very close to your expectation. If any color needs revision, open the image file in question in Photoshop, make the desired color adjustments, and make a new printer pdf of just that page, examining it carefully before sending it back to the printer.

Why so much attention to color fidelity? Same reason that even though 99% of your audience may not notice bad grammar, someone (besides you) will see and care that a tomato is too blue. Why lose that person?

There, now you've got your three strands braided together—the collaborative processes that keep you aligned with your client's perspective, the compositional strategies that make your creative work sing, and the production and quality-control habits that ensure that a well crafted design product results from all your hard work and insight.

Time to test that rope with some exercises.

FOUR EXERCISES

These four exercises are all designed as client-designer partnerships and are best done with a partner or in a group—though each can be done solo if no collaborator is available. The exercises begin with an exploration of the meaning and expression of brand, and progress through increasingly ambitious projects that allow participants to apply the concepts of coherence and complexity in developing prototype designs with attention to audience, outcome, message, and tone. Each exercise is based on the kinds of design processes and client interactions that designers typically experience in real life.

1. Develop a promotional campaign around
    a new product

2. Design a suite of book covers and sample
    interior pages

3. Create a brochure about a
    redevelopment project

4. Research and design a publication
    package about a travel destination

See page 77 for suggested ways to use these
exercises in classes or workshops.

But first . . .

BRAND: VERBISH NOUN OR NOUNISH VERB?

It's amusing that the glitzy multi-bazillion dollar global branding industry started with the mark that ranchers burn into a cow's haunch. The mode of presentation on Madison Avenue seems a world apart from *Bonanza*. And yet, in both cases, we're talking about a way of signifying "This belongs to me."

Over the years, the non-agricultural meaning of the term "brand" has evolved to denote something more than stamping a mark of ownership on livestock. The phrase "corporate brand" might suggest that a corporate logo is analogous to the scar on the cow. In a way, it is: both signify the identity of the owner, and over time, people come to associate the mark with their idea of who that owner is—in short, "brand" comes to mean not that act of putting a mark on a cow (the verb), but what a given entity means to the public (a noun). As a result, a corporate brand is not something easily changed with a hot poker; rather, it is an abstraction of the character of the associated organization. The mark is almost incidental—not the brand itself, but a reference to it. "This represents me."

There's a problem here if you're in the branding business: if the term "brand" is a noun describing the associations the public

has with a certain entity, there would seem to
be nothing left for a branding agency to do.
The brand is there already.

Fortunately for branding agencies,
companies are always bringing in new
leaders, and new leaders typically want to
signal their ascendancy: updated logos, new
taglines, revised colors, a ceremonial "launch"
of some kind. There's an entire industry built
on this internal corporate dynamic, which
goes back at least as far as to the pharaohs
re-carving previous pharaoh statues into their
own likenesses. Even though these exercises
are often called "re-brands," the brand doesn't
actually change, because the brand is rooted
not in what colors and slogans the new boss
likes, but in what the company more durably
means to its public. It's still a noun.

Perhaps it was this quandary that inspired the invention of the "Brand Promise."
This idea gives the agency more agency—a
way to focus on not what the brand is now,
but what it aspires to be: the noun of brand
thus regains its ability to also be a verb.
With brand aspirations identified, the agency
works with the client to aim toward those
aspirations, through a combination of revised
activities of the company itself, education
of the public as to the nature and purpose

of those revised activities, and careful
refinements of the graphic identity program
to support those aspirations. Without the
first two elements—that is, without real
change and public awareness of it—the
branding effort leaves a faint mark, if any.

This brings us around to this first
exercise, which will require the
designer to develop a logo that stands for
the brand of a new product. Since the
product is new, this brand is necessarily
aspirational, but for the effort to succeed,
the brand expression must align with the
real attributes of the product. If customers
feel disappointed or deceived, that negative
association becomes part of the brand.

The interview, therefore, is critical.
The designer must work with the client
to identify the audience, desired outcome,
message, and tone to make sure that what
the promotional campaign promises will
be delivered, and delivered to the right
audience of people who will understand
and appreciate it. The logo should, in a
simple and symbolic way, stand for both
the aspiration and the underlying substance
of the product; and the related promotional
materials must stick to those same themes.

Exercise 1

*Role-playing the client and designer to develop a
brand statement, design brief, logo, and simple
promotional campaign for a new product, event,
band, etc.*

Two meetings
1. Clients present products and clients and
designers collaboratively develop
brand statement and design brief
2. Designers present proposals for critique

Working time between
4–6 hours for each designer (working
simultaneously on each other's product)

First, put on your "client hat." Come up
with an idea for a product, event, band, etc.

You partner puts on the "designer hat"
and you work together to develop a brand
statement, summing up in a sentence or
two what the client and designer agree
that the product means to its audience/
user/customer. Next, they develop a design
brief (often also called a creative brief) that
spells out who is the target audience or
customer, what we hope they will do as a
result of exposure to the campaign, what

the message will be to encourage them to do that, and what the tone of the materials should be to support that message. It is up to the designer to take notes and get down all the information that comes out of the above discussions.

Then client and designer trade roles and do the same for the other person's product idea.

Deliverables from each designer
- Brand statement
- Design or creative brief
- Prototype logo that symbolizes the brand statement; present up to three options (note that developing and refining a real logo takes much, much longer)
- Three campaign options, each consisting of an 8.5 x 11-inch vertical magazine ad, a 6-foot x 18-foot horizontal billboard, and a 5 x 7-inch post card front (horizontal or vertical). Note that a full-page magazine ad must be set up with .125 bleeds and crop marks. Each of the campaigns should take a different approach. You can give each campaign idea a name if you like to make it easier to refer to it in discussion. Use the file setup protocols as described on pages 40–55.

Exercise 2

*Role play client and designer to create a suite of
book covers*

Two meetings
1. Each client presents three book titles and
synopsis of the plots; collaborate to develop
creative brief
2. Each designer presents proposals for
critique

Working time between
6–10 hours

Client selects three books or stories that are
thematically related to each other and
engages the designer to create a suite of
covers for the books that reflect the themes
and action of each text and also present the
group of books as a related series. Client
supplies summary of the books.

    Imagine that these three titles are
being released as a group, so the audience
should understand from common elements
across all three that the books are related
to each other. At the same time, each cover
should express what that story is about.
Your understanding of brand should come
into play here: What do this author and

these books mean to the public? And your approach should also, of course, answer the four questions around audience, outcome, message, and tone.

Design the front of each cover as well as the spine. Also design one or more internal pages that show the typography that will be used for the body text and how headings and page numbers will be treated (this should be the same across all three books, so only one sample is needed). You are creating an "umbrella brand" for the series as well as individual designs for each cover. Include a graphic (on the spine at least) denoting a thematically appropriate real or fictional publishing house.

Decisions you will need to make: what kind of imagery can effectively stand for the themes of the literature? What typeface(s) support that effort? Think about color, texture, contrast, and layout. And think about competing for visual attention in the context of shelves in bookstores as well as online situations.

Designer and client trade places and repeat.

Deliverables from each designer
- Creative brief
- 3 covers and internal page(s)

Use Photoshop and Illustrator as needed
for illustrations, but the book setup and
page layout must be done in InDesign
using the file setup protocols as described
on pages 40–55. The presentation should
be a pdf file including all three covers
and the sample interior pages, introduced
by a creative brief that demonstrates
significant understanding of the books and
their audience as well as a rationale for
the choices you have made in light of that
knowledge.

Exercise 3

Role play client and designer to first sketch a layout plan for a brochure about a top-secret redevelopment project, then follow through with an actual design after the real content is delivered.

Three meetings
1. Client presents general parameters
2. Designer shows prototype and client supplies actual text and images
3. Designer presents final design for critique

Working time between
4–6 hours between #1 and #2
6–10 hours between #2 and #3

The designer has been retained to design a brochure about a top-secret new real-estate development project. This project is so confidential that no text or images have been released, to prevent any possibility of anything leaking to the media. But the developers want to send a brochure design to a printer by the day after the project will be announced, so they have supplied the designer with a detailed list of what items will need to be included so that the designer can pre-block the layout and then swap in the real text and images at the last moment and send it to the printer.

The exact location of the site is unknown, but you do know it was used for something else previously—it could be a deserted military facility someplace, it could be a post-industrial "brownfield" site, it could be a neglected urban neighborhood, or something else. All you know about what will be built there is it will be used by a lot of people in a largely public setting.

Generic specifications

The brochure will need to fold down to 4 x 9 inches so it can squeeze into a #10 business envelope. It can be a stapled booklet, a flat sheet folded down to 4 x 9 made up of as many panels as necessary, or a combination of the two—or some other format, as long as it's 4 x 9 inches finished size. To keep the postage rate down, the total thickness can be no more than 8 sheets after folding. The paper is 100# text weight, either uncoated or coated.

The text to be included is as follows:

• Introductory text totaling 120 words. This should run in larger type.

- Additional 300 words of narrative text about the project (can run continuously or in chunks)
- Captions for each of 5 to 8 images, caption text ranging from 5 to 35 words.
- Brief quote from each of 5 persons, each quote ranging from 20 to 50 words.
- A graphic showing 5 years of past data relevant to the project.

Images to be included:
- A beautiful cover image
- 3 "before" images
- 5 to 8 "after" images (artist renderings and photos of similar projects), including a map
- Portraits of the 5 people quoted

Your job is to create a dummy brochure that has space set aside for all these elements. You can do this using gray boxes for the images, or you can find pictures that work for you and obviously mark them "FPO" (For Position Only). Assume that everything provided to you will be of high resolution and good quality.

For the text, use Lorem Ipsum "dummy text" as needed. Come up with a preliminary type specification for at least the following: a cover headline, section titles, intro text, body text, captions, and the data chart. Define each of these as a paragraph style, so when you get all the real text delivered to you under deadline, you can get it all in there and properly specified in a hurry. Use the file setup protocols as described on pages 40–55.

The Client's Job
Pick a site for the hypothetical project and write the text and gather images:
- An overview paragraph (not for inclusion in the design) that identifies the site and explains what is to be built there.
- Introductory text totaling 120 words. This should run in larger type.
- Additional 300 words of narrative text about the project (can run continuously or in chunks)
- Captions for each of 5 to 8 images, caption text ranging from 5 to 35 words.
- Brief quote from each of 5 persons, each quote ranging from 20 to 50 words.
- 5 years of past data relevant to the project for the designer to make graphics

Images to be included:

- A beautiful cover image
- 3 "before" images
- 5 to 8 "after" images (artist renderings
  and photos of similar projects), including
  a rough map
- Portraits of the 5 people quoted

Sequence

When the designer has completed the
dummy brochure, the client supplies the
actual text and images. The map should be
a rough sketch on a napkin or a bad online
capture—something where the designer will
have to actually draw or otherwise create
a map. Similarly, the data should be just
numbers, not in graphic form. The designer
should expect to make some modifications
to the brochure's blocked layout and/or type
specifications in response to the content
and tone of the real text and images.
A brief discussion should identify the
audience, outcome, message, and tone.

Deliverable from each designer:

A draft complete brochure should be
delivered within 24 hours after copy and
images are received. Specify the paper type.

This brochure exercise poses a number of
real-world-type challenges, such as needing
to have a design pretty well started before
any real content arrives and needing to
work under extreme deadline pressure.
It requires skills designers often find
useful: how to design attractive and useful
information graphics and how to make
maps that are attuned to that specific
publication and its audience.

It also illustrates how the humble
folded brochure, simple as it may seem,
can actually be one of the more challenging
design forms to work with because it
can be so hard to predict how users will
unfold and otherwise manipulate the
piece, especially if the format is a large
single sheet folded down in a certain way.
Working out these logistics is a good reason
to start early on any folded-paper project.

The role-playing aspect is particularly
involved here; this helps the designer
understand the client's perspective and vice
versa, and that mutual understanding can
help in future collaborations.

Exercise 4

Client and designer collaborate to research and design a publication package (graphic identity, magazine, poster) about a travel destination

Three meetings
1. Client identifies destination; collaborate to develop creative brief
2. Designer presents preliminary design sketch for review; client provides update of some info due to late-breaking news—this necessitates some revisions
3. Designer presents final design

Working time between
8–12 hours between #1 and #2
4–6 hours between #2 and #3

First, pick a travel destination. It can be in the USA or in another country, rural, urban, etc. You have been hired by that place's tourism bureau to develop some materials for visitors. Client supplies:

- introductory text
- three articles, each about one of the area's main attractions or activities
- listings information about hotels, restaurants, shopping, and attractions
- data to be used in graphics
- a selection of photos with captions

Deliverables from each designer:

1. a simple graphic identity for the travel destination that supports its "brand promise"

2. a magazine of 16 to 24 pages

3. a poster up to 24 x 36 inches, suitable for framing

Graphic identity must include:

- a logo
- a typographic specification to be used throughout printed materials: headlines, subheads, body copy, listings, and caption style
- a color palette of at least 3 colors
- a brand statement that spells out audience, goals, message, and tone for the identity program. "Brand promise" is aspirational—not only what the audience feels already about this travel destination, but what you and the client want them to feel. Your identity program helps project that aspiration.

Magazine must include:

- front and back covers
- introductory text
- at least three article sections, each about one of the area's main attractions or activities
- at least one map of the place (with inset maps if applicable)
- listings information about hotels, restaurants, shopping, and attractions
- 3 ads, one full-page, one half-page, one quarter-page. By strange coincidence, these are the same ads developed earlier in exercise #1. Mix your partner's ads and your own
- at least one presentation of data about the place

Poster must include:

- just a poster, a really great poster

Verification of production specs:
Use the file setup protocols as described on pages 40–55. Provide a screencap of links palette with marks noting any images of inadequate resolution or not in CMYK color space. Provide a pdf of one page exported to printer specifications with crop marks and showing proper bleeds.

Files delivered:
- 1 pdf file describing the brand identity, including logo, type spec, colors, and statement
- 1 pdf file for the entire magazine
- 1 pdf file for the poster
- 1 jpeg screen capture showing links palette
- 1 pdf of a single page showing pdf export at printer specifications

Now plan your vacation and go!

**Suggested uses of these exercises in
classes and workshops**

Exercise #1 can be condensed and used
on its own for a single-day workshop,
with participants pairing off in client and
designer roles. If the setting has computers
with design software and internet access,
design sketches can be done using
InDesign. Or the exercise can be paper-
only, with creative briefs written down
and logo ideas sketched by hand. Allow
45 minutes for each role with a 15-minute
break between, then 45 minutes for sharing
and discussion with the other participants.

In a longer-format class setting, structure
each exercise as a "meet-and-go-away"
process where the designer takes meeting
input home and comes back in a week
with a design response. Use class time for
the team meetings and broader discussion.
Over the course of a quarter or semester,
therefore, allow two weeks for each of the
first two exercises, and three weeks for each
of the second two, for a total of 10 weeks.
The instructor would cover other related
topics in and around those projects.

SIDEWAYS BIBLIOGRAPHY

All the famous graphic designers who ever lived either wrote books or have had books written about them. If there's a designer whose work you like, a book is almost certain to exist. Find it and read it. Graphic design books aren't listed in this bibliography because where would you stop? Certainly someone's feelings would be hurt.

So these are titles that touch on the themes of this book from the outside—the list doesn't drill deep into the world of graphic design, but looks sideways. A few are about urban design or architecture, some about visual or musical aesthetics, some about how humans seem to operate.

Aschenbrenner, Karl. *The Concept of Coherence in Art*. Dordrecht, Netherlands: D. Reidel Publishing Company, 1983.

Bringhurst, Robert. *The Elements of Typographic Style*, Fourth edition: Vancouver, BC: Hartley & Marks, 2012.

Csikszentimihalyi, Mihaly, and Isabella Selega Csikszentimihalyi, eds. *Optimal Experience: Psychological Studies of Flow in Consciousness*. New York: Cambridge University Press, 1988.

Hiss, Tony. *The Experience of Place*. New York: Alfred A. Knopf, 1990.

Jacobs, Jane. *The Death and Life of Great American Cities*. New York: Random House, 1961.

Lynch, Kevin. *The Image of the City*. Cambridge: M.I.T. Press, 1960.

Munro, Thomas H. *Form and Style in the Arts: An Introduction to Aesthetic Morphology*. Cleveland: Press of Case Western Reserve University, 1970.

O'Gieblyn, Meghan. *God, Human, Animal, Machine: Technology, Metaphor, and the Search for Meaning.* New York: Doubleday, 2021.

Shakespeare, William. *The Complete Works of William Shakespeare.* Various publishers, 1589– .

Toch, Ernst. *The Shaping Forces in Music: An Enquiry into Harmony, Melody, Counterpoint, Form.* Los Angeles: Criterion Music Group, 1948.

Tufte, Edward R. *Envisioning Information,* Cheshire, CT: Graphics Press, 1990.

Wilson, Edward O. *Consilience: The Unity of Knowledge.* New York: Alfred A. Knopf, 1998.

Venturi, Robert. *Complexity and Contradiction in Architecture.* New York: The Museum of Modern Art, 1966.

Typefaces:
Perpetua Titling
DIN 2014 Narrow
Marion

Independent authors rely on reader reviews to spread the word about their publications.
If you like this book, please leave a review detailing why on your favorite platform(s), such as Goodreads, Amazon, Barnes & Noble, and/or Bookshop.org.

Thank you!

Also by G. M. Donley
Available at online retailers or through your favorite local bookshop

Crombie Hill
A novel

"A captivating blend of literary prose and historical fiction . . . lyrical and immersive . . . a timeless meditation on the connections that bind us together across generations."
—Goodreads/A Look Inside (4 stars)

"The emotions, human drama and intelligence kept me propelled through the whole thing."
—Goodreads (5 stars)

Night Music
Images from dark and noisy places in Cleveland

"Donley's images convey the visceral experience of being at a show in a small, closely packed room: the vibrations of the sound, the flare of the lights, the smell of the crowd, the humidity of the room."
—Anastasia Pantsios, journalist and photographer, CoolCleveland.com, Scene, Free Times, Plain Dealer.

The Legend of Castle Cove
A novel

The Virtues of Alignment
Stories and not stories

www.ingramcontent.com/pod-product-compliance
Lightning Source LLC
Chambersburg PA
CBHW021125130726
47988CB00003B/1178